Native American Lives

Ella Cara Deloria

Dakota Language Protector

Written by Diane Wilson

Illustrated by Tashia Hart

Minnesota Humanities Center

Lerner Publications ◆ Minneapolis

GENEROUSLY SUPPORTED BY

This book has been supported by the Minnesota Humanities Center, generously funded through the Shakopee Mdewakanton Sioux Community (SMSC) through its Understand Native Minnesota campaign, also funded in part by the Arts and Cultural Heritage Fund that was created with the vote of the people of Minnesota on November 4, 2008, and the National Endowment for the Humanities.

Lerner Publications Company
An imprint of Lerner Publishing Group, Inc.
241 First Avenue North
Minneapolis, MN 55401 USA

For reading levels and more information, look up this title at www.lernerbooks.com.

Illustration credits: Tashia Hart
Additional image credits: family photos courtesy of Philip J. Deloria, back cover, p. 6; Laura Westlund, p. 21; Wikimedia Commons PD, p. 26; *Drawing* by Mary Sully, photo provided by Stephen Petegorsky/Mary Sully Foundation, p. 29; Anastasiia Gecko/Shutterstock (background pattern).

Main body text set in Noto Serif. Typeface provided by Google Open Source.

Library of Congress Cataloging-in-Publication Data

Names: Wilson, Diane, 1954– author. | Hart, Tashia, illustrator.
Title: Ella Cara Deloria : Dakota language protector / written by Diane Wilson ; illustrated by Tashia Hart.
Description: Minneapolis : Lerner Publications, 2026. | Series: Native American lives | Includes bibliographical references and index. | Audience: Ages 9–14. | Audience: Grades 4–6. | Summary: "Ella Cara Deloria was a Dakota ethnographer and linguist. She recorded the stories of Indigenous peoples. From protecting the Dakota language to writing books and more, her incredible life is sure to inspire young readers"— Provided by publisher.
Identifiers: LCCN 2024045566 (print) | LCCN 2024045567 (ebook) | ISBN 9798765671788 (paperback) | ISBN 9798765679890 (epub)
Subjects: LCSH: Deloria, Ella Cara—Juvenile literature. | Linguists—United States—Biography—Juvenile literature. | Ethnologists—United States—Biography—Juvenile literature. | Dakota Indians—Biography—Juvenile literature. | Dakota women—Biography—Juvenile literature. | Dakota language—Juvenile literature. | LCGFT: Biographies.
Classification: LCC P85.D46 W55 2025 (print) | LCC P85.D46 (ebook) | DDC 497/.52430092 [B]—dc23/eng/20241024

LC record available at https://lccn.loc.gov/2024045566
LC ebook record available at https://lccn.loc.gov/2024045567

Manufactured in the United States of America
1-1011607-54280-11/25/2024

Table of Contents

Introduction

Storytelling, a traditional tool of many Indigenous peoples, is alive and well among Native Americans of many nations. The authors, illustrators, and editors of this series, who are all Dakota or Ojibwe, continue their cultural traditions in creating these books and telling stories of leaders, athletes, teachers, and artists.

This series of books is by, for, and about Dakota and Anishinaabe (Ojibwe) and other Indigenous peoples. In portraying our histories, knowledge ways, culture keepers, and beloved figures, these biographies help Dakota, Anishinaabe, and other Native American children imagine their own potential for full futures.

We prefer to be called by our tribal names (Dakota, Ojibwe, or Anishinaabe) or "Native American" or "Indigenous." We use "Indian" in

numerous contexts today, such as the "National Museum of the American Indian." In this series, you will see the use of the term "Indian" in historical context, and not as a derogatory name.

We hope readers will consider how the facts of social barriers based on race, culture, education, and class are part of the life stories in these books. History, especially the impacts of treaties, underlies these stories as well. The legacy of forced education in the English language by government and religious schools, poverty, and the disruption of family life are also themes. The Indigenous peoples featured in these narratives overcame such circumstances. Natural talent in art and sports, leadership skills, and Native American cultural strengths are also themes of their stories.

This series includes stories of historical figures who lived, worked, and broke barriers a hundred years ago, as well as the ongoing accomplishments of exceptional Ojibwe and Dakota people who became leaders, athletes, teachers, and artists, and whose life stories are meaningful today. Our hope is that you see yourselves in the extraordinary lives presented in these books.

—Gwen N. Westerman and Heid E. Erdrich,
series editors, May 2024

Ella Cara Deloria

Aŋpetu Waŝte Wiŋ

"Beautiful Day Woman"

Chapter 1

The Dakota Way of Life

When Ella Cara Deloria was a young girl, she lived on the Standing Rock Reservation in South Dakota. She was a good student who loved to read. She especially enjoyed visiting with the grandfathers and grandmothers who lived nearby. With her warm smile and good manners, Ella would have been a welcomed guest. She listened closely to them and learned the stories of their people.

Ella's grandfather, Saswe, was born in 1816. Back then, the Dakota people moved from camp to camp as they followed the bison. These large animals are sometimes called buffalo. Millions of bison roamed the plains. Some bison weighed up to 2,000 pounds (907 kg). When they stampeded across the land, it sounded like thunder.

Dakota families honored the buffalo as relatives who gave their lives so the people could survive. They used buffalo hides to make tipis, blankets, and winter coats. A single buffalo provided many pounds of meat that the Dakotas could roast or dry for winter. The Dakotas used buffalo bones to make tools such as needles and garden hoes, and they used ribs to make sleds for children to play with.

Through the long winters, the Dakota people watched groups of stars move across the sky. As these constellations changed, the people knew when to move to their summer camps. The Seven Sisters constellation showed them when to plant their corn and squash. Astronomers also call this constellation the Pleiades.

During this time, the Dakotas did not need books or a written language. Instead, they saved their history by telling oral stories. Each year, or winter, had a name and a story about a memorable event that happened. The Dakotas called these stories winter counts, and they repeated the stories many times so the stories would not be forgotten.

Remembering so many stories is not easy. A good storyteller is like an actor who can make people laugh or cry. In Saswe's time, some storytellers could remember three hundred winter counts!

A family might offer a feast and gifts to a storyteller who shares these stories with the children. The ohuŋkaŋkaŋ are very old stories about spirit beings, such as the trickster Iktomi. Others are about family life and how things came to be on this earth.

Saswe was raised this way as a Dakota boy. Almost as soon as he could talk, he learned kinship terms. These terms are a polite way of speaking to each family member instead of calling them by their names. Saswe called his father Até and his mother Ina. Saswe knew his father's brother would be like another father, and his mother's sister would be like another mother. Saswe's uncles and aunts helped him through his life. The Dakota people lived closely together in camps, and these kinship rules helped everyone get along and know their families.

Dakota children grew up in a large family, surrounded by aunts, uncles, grandparents, grandchildren, and cousins. This extended family, or tioṡpaye, helped teach each child important skills. The men taught boys how to ride horses, hunt and fish, and fight when necessary. Girls learned from their mothers and aunts to care for the home and garden, gather plants, and raise children. Girls and boys were equally important to their community. Everyone learned the stories and rules, and everyone had a role in their community.

When Saswe was a young man, he had a vision. In his dream, he had to choose between two roads. One road showed four generations who would

prosper but give nothing to the world. The other, the Red Road, would be dangerous but filled with great opportunities. Saswe chose the Red Road and learned how to use plant medicines and become a healer for his people.

Saswe's dream showed him his life in a new way. He knew the world was changing, and his family would have to change with it.

Chapter 2

Learning New Ways

By 1850, European immigrants and Americans were moving into the Dakota homeland. They brought new ideas and a desire for land that threatened the Dakota way of life. The railroads brought hunters who slaughtered millions of bison for sport and profit until the bison were nearly extinct. Unlike the Dakota hunters, these people killed for hides and trophies, and left the meat to rot. Without the bison, Dakota families would not have enough food.

In 1858, the United States government made agreements called treaties with the Dakota people. In exchange for food and payments, the Dakotas were supposed to live and hunt in smaller areas called reservations. The government also wanted the Dakotas to live in houses and learn to farm like the settlers. Many churches sent missionaries to teach the Dakotas to become Christians. The missionaries did not understand that these Dakota men and women had their own spiritual beliefs and did not want to give them up.

Saswe wanted to help his people learn to live in this changing world. In 1873, he chose to become a Christian in the Episcopal Church. The church gave him a new name: Francis Deloria. His family began to follow both traditional Dakota and Christian beliefs. Saswe's son, Tipi Sapa, had grown up helping him gather plants for medicine for his relatives. Now, living on the Yankton reservation, Saswe had to find another way to serve his people.

When Tipi Sapa was seventeen, the Episcopal Mission on the reservation invited him to live with him. The minister and mission teachers repeatedly asked Tipi Sapa to cut his hair, dress like an American, and go to school. Each time, he said no. Finally, after many talks with the minister and his father, he agreed. Tipi Sapa believed it was the best way to help his people, but it also meant he had to face their disapproval.

"Coward. He fears warfare," they said. "See, he chooses an easy life."

It was not easy for Tipi Sapa to hear these insults. He decided to change his name. From then on, Tipi Sapa was called Philip Deloria. He went to college for two years, then returned to his reservation and worked at different churches. In 1885, he went to work at St. Elizabeth's Church on the Standing Rock Reservation. Sometimes he wrote his sermon by spending Saturday afternoons lying on the ground, watching clouds. He hoped studying the clouds would help him shape his thoughts into powerful words.

Philip now believed the Dakotas should give up their traditional ways and join the church. At Standing Rock, he met Akicita Wiŋ, whose English name was Mary Sully Bordeaux. Her father was Alfred Sully, a general in the US Army. Mary's mother, Pehaŋdutawiŋ, raised her as a traditional Dakota girl on the Yankton Reservation. Philip and Mary married in 1888.

Ella was born in 1889 as strong blizzard winds blew heavy snow across the Yankton Reservation. Her parents named her Aŋpetu Waṡte Wiŋ, Beautiful Day Woman, making a joke about the weather. Her sister, Susan, was born in 1896. Susan would grow up

to become a talented artist like her great-grandfather, Thomas Sully. In 1901, Ella's brother, Vine, was born. He would become a well-known priest, like his father. The Deloria children grew up speaking Dakota as their first language at home.

Near the church at Standing Rock, Philip helped start St. Elizabeth's Mission School in 1886. In its early days, only a few Dakota children came. Many of their families did not want to become Christians. Thirty years later, the US government forced the Dakota people, through treaties, to give up most of their homeland. The US government often did not uphold the treaties and pay the Dakota what was owed them. No longer able to hunt for themselves, they had to rely on the government for food. They were angry at being cheated and afraid of losing their way of life.

Like her father, Ella would need to find a new way to help her people.

Chapter 3

Living in Two Cultures

Just as Saswe had foreseen, learning these different ways of life helped the Deloria family survive. It also meant that Ella grew up in two cultures.

Ella lived with her family in a big white house on a hill, not far from the Episcopal church and St. Elizabeth's school. Below the hill, Dakota families often camped in tipis for several days. They came to visit with other families, pick up their food, and go to church.

Even as a child, Ella was fascinated by the stories she heard from her family. Her father and his friends enjoyed sharing stories of the past. When her parents traveled for church business, Ella's grandmother would set up her tipi in their yard. Her grandmother

often told stories while caring for the children. Ella's mother and aunts also shared stories about the Dakota way of life with her.

Sometimes Ella would sneak away to the nearby camp to listen to the Lakota storytellers. Her family would find her sitting at a campfire, her moccasins tucked beneath her long cotton dress. As an adult, Ella remembered keeping her eyes and ears open so she could remember all she ever saw and heard of her Dakota life. At this camp, she learned the Teton dialect of Lakota, which was closely related to her Dakota language.

Ella was baptized as a Christian and spoke English at school where the teachers expected her to act differently than she would at home. When she was older, Ella wrote that this was a confusing way to grow up.

Life at St. Elizabeth's school was demanding. Students learned to read and write English, take care of the animals, cut hay, and chop wood. The girls helped cook and do laundry in big tubs. They also worked in the garden and grew vegetables for the kitchen. They went to the nearby rivers and hauled water in barrels back to the school. They used lamps filled with kerosene, a flammable oil, and traveled by horse or wagon.

Map of Dakota Dialects

The Santee, or Eastern Dakota, live near the lakes and woods along the Minnesota River and Red River, and speak the Dakota dialect. The Yankton Dakota live on the prairies and speak both Dakota and Nakota dialects. The Teton, or Western Dakota, live on the plains and speak the Lakota dialect. These groups make up the Oceti Ṡakowiŋ (oh-cheh-tee shah-koh-ween).

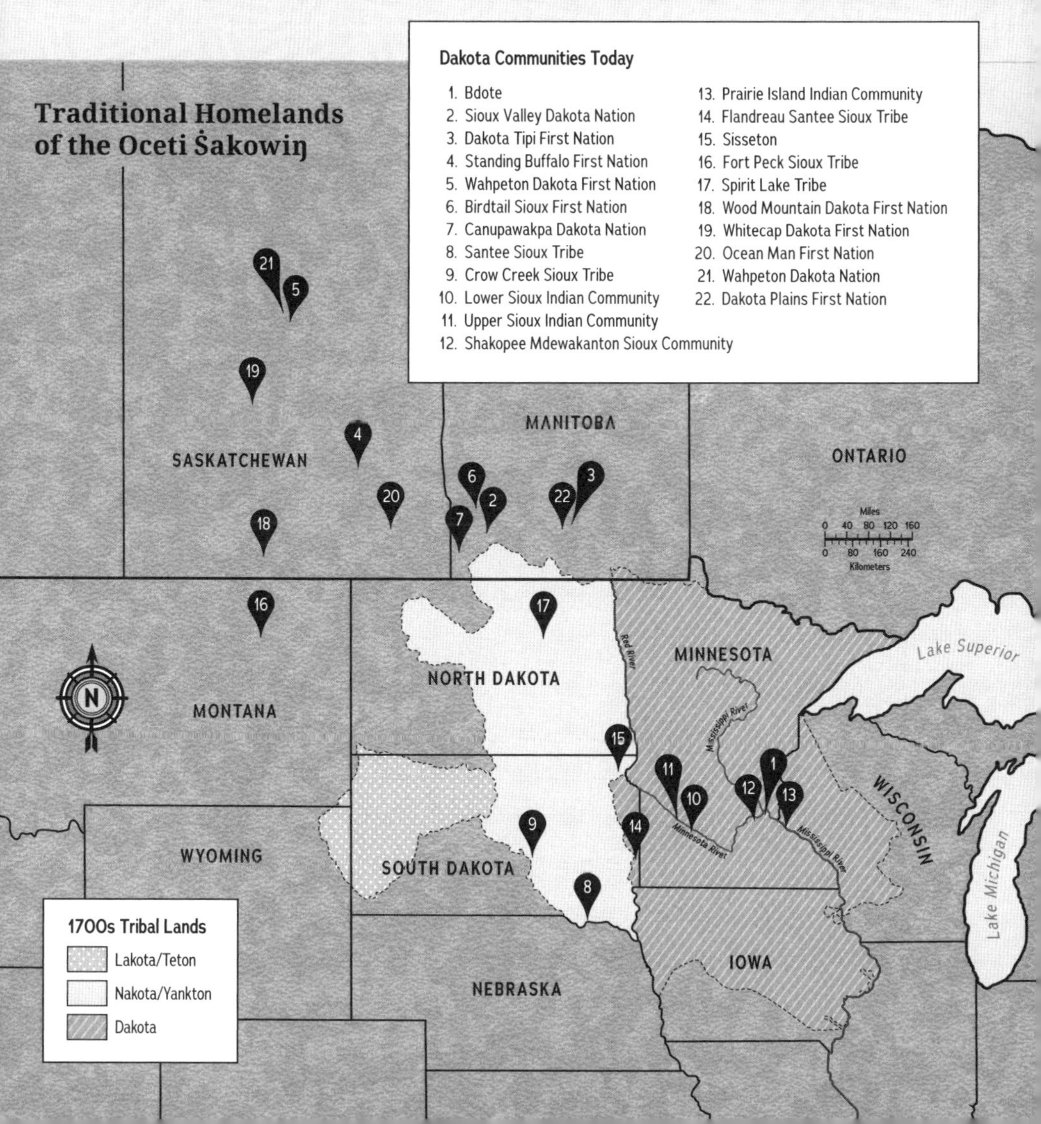

The older girls, including Ella, helped the young ones learn English. One little boy named Frank had a hard time learning to say the Lord's Prayer, a Christian prayer, in English. While practicing with Ella, he sometimes slipped back into Lakota. She wanted to laugh, but instead, she treated him with kindness so he would keep practicing English. Ella was already learning to become a teacher and mentor like her teacher Miss Mary Francis, who encouraged her lifelong love of reading and writing.

When Ella was twelve, she was strong enough to drive a team of horses pulling a wagon. Once, while she was helping her father, something spooked the horses. They took off running! The wagon tipped, throwing Ella to the ground. She hurt her right thumb, and it had to be removed. This accident made typing difficult for the rest of her life, but Ella did not let it slow her down. She was always an active girl, playing games, dancing, and helping with chores.

One morning, Ella fell asleep while sitting in a pew at her father's church. She dreamed that she was both a boy and a girl. She took money from her father, went off to another land, and met other people. At the end of the dream, Ella crossed the river and came back. Her father forgave her for taking the money, and her family welcomed her home. Over the years, Ella often thought about the meaning of this dream. It seemed to be telling her about the work she was supposed to do.

When she was fourteen, Ella went to Sioux Falls, South Dakota, to attend All Saints School, a private boarding school. Most of the girls there were the daughters of Episcopal ministers. This was her first time living away from home. Her cheerful personality helped her make friends. She did well in her classes, especially English and Latin. She was excited and nervous to be so far away from her family. In her last year at All Saints, she wrote an essay that won her a scholarship to attend Oberlin College in Ohio.

Chapter 4
Leaving Home

Attending Oberlin College was a big step for Deloria. In 1910, she was one of the very few Dakota women to go to college. But twenty-one-year-old Deloria was ready for this opportunity. She was a hard worker and hungry to learn.

Deloria did so well at Oberlin that she transferred to the Teachers College at Columbia University in New York. She traveled there with Susan. With so many tall buildings, the city was unlike anything they had ever seen before. Deloria said that New York was a place where the cement seemed endless, where she did not feel connected to the earth. But the university offered new ways for her to keep learning.

At Columbia, she met Franz Boas. He was a

well-known professor who taught anthropology, the study of human beings. She did not know that meeting him would change her life. He hired her to help his students learn the Lakota language, and she earned her very first paycheck. She was paid $18 a month, which is about $460 today.

Deloria enjoyed studying at the university, but she realized many people knew little about her Dakota relatives. Some scholars had written articles about Dakota life that were not correct. She worried these mistakes would create more wrong ideas and harmful government policies. Life was already hard for the Dakota people. She wondered if she could help by sharing what she knew about Dakota culture.

When Deloria graduated in 1915, Native peoples were not American citizens, nor were they allowed to vote. Their spiritual practices were illegal. Native peoples were treated as inferior to other Americans. At the time, no women in the US were allowed to vote.

Deloria's first teaching job was at her old school, All Saints. After Susan graduated from there in 1916, the sisters immediately went home to care for their sick mother. Their mother died a short time later, and Deloria knew she needed to help her family. Deloria took care of Susan and Vine and helped their father with his church work. She also needed to find a way to earn money to support them.

Susan Deloria, also known as artist Mary Sully, ca. 1912

In 1918, the two sisters returned to New York. There, Deloria worked as the national health education secretary of the YWCA, traveling to reservation schools around the country. Then, in 1923, the Haskell Institute in Lawrence, Kansas, hired her to teach physical education to Native girls. She coached sports, taught dancing, and served as a substitute teacher.

Unlike her father, Deloria believed that Dakota people did not have to give up who they were to be Americans. In a speech to students at St. Mary's Indian School for Girls in Springfield, South Dakota, she encouraged them to learn to live with both cultures. She also told them how having endurance and persistence leads to success. She repeated this idea throughout her life.

To help other teachers understand more about Dakota people, Deloria wrote and produced two pageants. These all-day celebrations included opening ceremonies, games and contests, dances, and feasts. She discovered she had a talent for writing!

While Deloria was at Haskell, she received a letter. Boas remembered when Deloria taught his students about the Lakota language. He wanted to know if she would help with a translation project. She had enjoyed the work and agreed to help. She was about to begin the work she cared about most.

Chapter 5
Becoming a Storyteller

As Deloria's life was about to change, the federal government was changing the way it treated Native peoples. A report showed that many people on reservations were poor. The government had taken children away from their families and sent them to federal off-reservation boarding schools. Those children came home as strangers and were often not accepted as part of the community. The tiośpaye and kinship system were falling apart. The Dakota way of life was in danger of disappearing.

Living on her reservation, Deloria saw the harm done by these schools where students were forbidden to speak their languages. Many students would no longer or could no longer speak their languages after

leaving these schools. Fewer children were raised speaking the Dakota language. As grandparents died, so did the stories and traditions they knew, and there were no new speakers to take their place.

She knew that if Dakota families lost their language and stories, they would lose the heart of their culture. How would the Dakota people remember who they were?

In 1928, Deloria returned to New York to work with Boas. Susan was in poor health and could not live on her own, so she became Deloria's companion and drove her wherever she needed to go. Susan was also a talented artist who worked with her sister on many projects. Using the name Mary Sully, she created hundreds of colored-pencil drawings about famous people. She called these drawings "Personality Prints."

PHOTO CREDIT: STEPHEN PETEGORSKY

Untitled drawing by Mary Sully

Boas wanted Deloria to help him translate many pages of Lakota stories into English. George Bushotter, a Teton Dakota, had collected these stories in 1887 for the US National Museum, which today is known as the Smithsonian Museum. Over time, Boas trained her to use scientific methods for recording languages and stories. She learned to keep detailed records. Deloria became one of the first Native ethnologists in the country. As an ethnologist, she studied the language and culture of the Dakota people.

Deloria said she wanted to study Dakota life as deeply as she could to find out where it would hurt Dakota people to lose cultural ways. Through her work, she learned the skills she needed to help preserve the Dakota language and culture. Finally, Deloria knew the meaning of her dream. She had found a way to help her people.

Over the next fifteen years, Deloria worked with Boas as his research assistant. She also translated Lakota and Dakota texts into English. She became friends with other women who had studied with Boas. One of them, Margaret Mead, became a famous anthropologist. Another well-known anthropologist, Ruth Benedict, helped Deloria with her research and writing.

Deloria often traveled between New York and South Dakota. Living in the city showed her a fast-paced new world. But South Dakota was always her home. She missed her family and her many Dakota friends. She enjoyed the work but struggled to support herself and her family. Boas helped raise money to pay her, but sometimes she had to work without pay.

After she finished translating the Bushotter stories, Deloria worked on the manuscripts of George Sword, a Teton Dakota, and Jack Frazier, a Santee Dakota. She wrote papers that gave true information about Dakota culture. Deloria and Boas together wrote an article on language that was published in 1933. She began to get national recognition for her work as a linguist and ethnologist.

As Deloria became well known, she never changed the way she treated people. She cared about everyone she met. Many people called her Aunt Ella and described her as charming and kind. Throughout her life, she always tried to be a good relative.

Chapter 6
Preserving Dakota Language

Deloria often gave speeches to groups who enjoyed her lively stories about Dakota life. Like her brother, Vine, she was a gifted speaker. Her stories showed how kinship rules had worked in her community. She shared her passion for the language by explaining the meaning of certain words. She let her audiences know that there was much more to tell and encouraged them to invite her back. Deloria entertained them while making sure they learned true information about the Dakota.

Throughout her life, Deloria thought the teachers and preachers who came to the reservations assumed the Dakotas had "no rules of life, no social organization, no ideals." She knew that was not true. The work she was doing to show who the Dakota are made her happy. "I actually feel that I have a mission," she said, "to make the Dakota people understandable, as human beings."

One of the projects she cared about was recording stories from Teton Lakota and Dakota communities. Over several years, she traveled across reservations looking for the oldest and most knowledgeable storytellers. She searched for people who remembered the ohuŋkaŋkaŋ, the stories she heard as a child.

Rather than taking notes, Deloria listened carefully and wrote them down later. Like a good storyteller, she needed a well-trained memory to do this work. Other times, she typed the stories on her typewriter as they were told to her. Her method was to write the story down directly as the storytellers related them to her. Then she translated the story into English, just as it was said in Lakota. Finally, she wrote another version of the story, so the meaning was the same in English.

Deloria published sixty-four of these stories as *Dakota Texts* in 1932. Her book is now considered to be one of the most important books written about the oral stories of the Teton Dakota. If she had not recorded these stories, they might have been lost as the storytellers passed away. Deloria's one regret was not having enough money to publish more of the stories she collected.

In 1934, Congress passed the Indian Reorganization Act. The US government realized its policies had not helped Native peoples. In many instances, these policies harmed Native peoples, especially in education where military-like rules and physical punishments for even very young children were common. The act made many changes that were supposed to make Native peoples' lives better. Especially important, it gave the Native tribes control of Indian education and closed many of the remaining federal off-reservation boarding schools. It also led to reforms in boarding schools that made them less harsh environments for children.

The world was very different from the one Deloria had known as a child. She wanted more than ever to save the language and stories that were disappearing.

Chapter 7
Staying True to Herself

Just as Deloria's career was going well, her family had more money trouble. Vine was just entering the ministry. He was paid half as much as the white priests and could not help care for their father. Deloria often talked about money with Boas. She did not think it was fair that she was paid less than white researchers.

Boas did not always understand the challenges Deloria faced in her life. "I live in my car," she wrote to him. "All our things are in it. And if I go anywhere, I find it cheapest to go in my car, and take my sister with me. I love her. I cannot do otherwise than give her a home of sorts." Even with his help, she often did not have enough money to support her family.

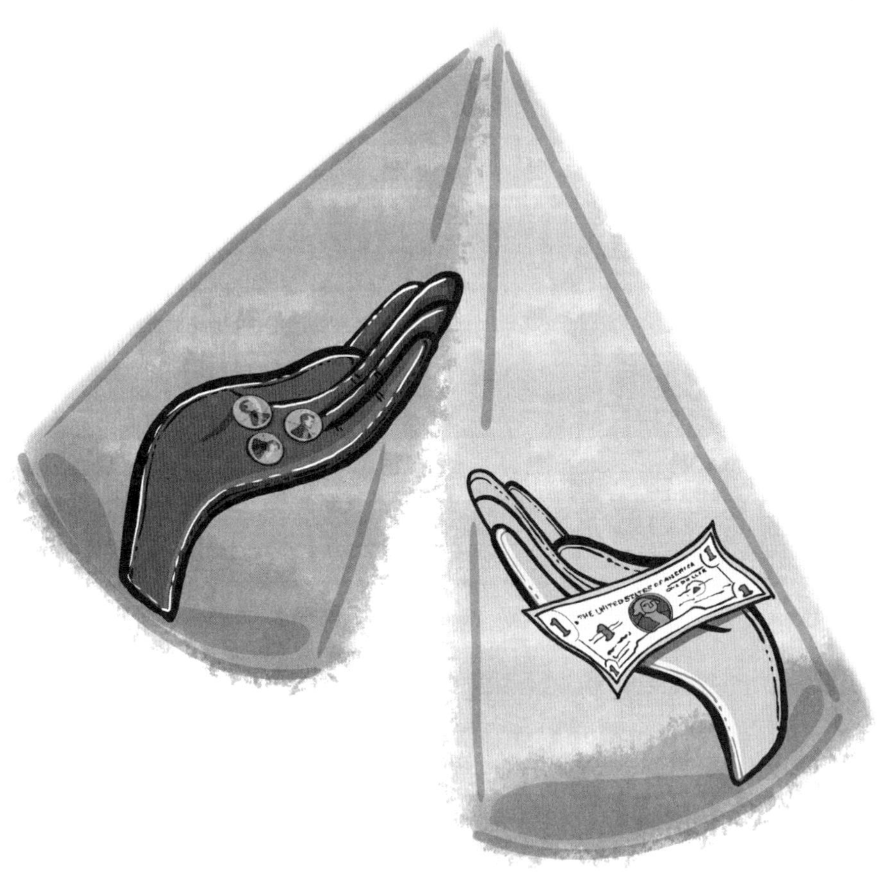

True to her Dakota teachings, she did not care about owning things. She and Susan often traveled in an old or borrowed car with her typewriter in the trunk. Sometimes she rented a hotel room or stayed with Vine. Without a place of her own, Deloria's files were sometimes lost or damaged. Still, she took notes anytime she met Dakota people who were willing to share their stories. Over the years, she gathered the largest collection of stories of any tribe.

No matter how hard her life became, her love of family was at the heart of her work. She never regarded them as a burden. She cared for her father throughout his long illness. Before he died in 1931, he often shared stories with her. He taught her about continuing the Dakota way of life, such as bringing food and gifts to the people she interviewed.

Deloria firmly believed that being a Dakota woman was helpful for her research. People trusted her to be careful with their information. She tried to explain to Boas why this was important. “If I go, bearing a gift, and gladden the hearts of the informants, and eat with them, and call them by the correct social kinship terms, then later I can go back, and ask them all sorts of questions, and get my information, as one would get favors from a relative,” she wrote. “It is hard to explain, but it is the only way I can work.”

In the university world, some scholars did not like Deloria because she was a Native woman. They said she couldn’t be fair when studying Native peoples. When she found mistakes in the earlier work of white scholars, they ignored her. They said she wasn’t well trained because she didn’t have a degree in anthropology. While Boas was a trusted mentor to her, even he did not always believe in her work. Despite their disagreements, Deloria respected him as a friend. Together, they published *Dakota Grammar* in 1941.

Deloria found new ways to use her skills by helping other Native communities. In 1940, the Bureau of Indian Affairs asked her to help the Lumbee Indians in Pembroke, North Carolina. They had lost most of their history and language. She and Susan produced two pageants for the Lumbee about their early days as a tribe. Susan created artwork and painted the sets.

The Lumbee women told Deloria the names of plants and animals, the foods they cooked, and the plant medicines they used. She collected over three hundred words and phrases on little cards. She kept her notes in big traveling trunks in a rented storage place in Fort Lee, Virginia. Sadly, when she could not pay her overdue rent, her trunks were sold to pay her bill. Her work on the

Lumbee language was lost and never completed.

During World War II, Deloria published her book, *Speaking of Indians*. At the time "Indian" was used more commonly than today. She wrote about Dakota people for white, Christian readers. She explained kinship rules and the importance of not caring too much about owning things. "If you wished to honor me publicly, you did not load me down personally with presents," she wrote. "You made someone else glad in my name." She dedicated *Speaking of Indians* to the memory of her beloved teacher, Miss Mary.

In her own life, Deloria lived according to this teaching. She never stopped working or trying to make life better for her family and her people.

Chapter 8
Being a Good Relative

As a scholar who also loved writing, Deloria sometimes got tired of scientific rules. There was so much more she wanted to say about Dakota people. She wanted to show how kinship worked in daily life. She especially wanted to write about the traditional roles of Dakota women, and how they served their people as leaders, healers, and storytellers.

Before Deloria, most histories about Dakota people had been written by white men. These men often believed women's work was less important than men's work. They rarely wrote about the role Dakota women played in their communities. When Europeans came, Native women were nearly erased from history. Deloria knew that women taught language and culture to their children and were honored for the important roles they held in the tioṡpaye. The Dakota people survived because women passed this knowledge to the next generation.

The study of anthropology began to change. Anthropologists realized people might learn more about other cultures by reading stories or novels instead of academic papers. In 1942, Deloria began working on her novel, *Waterlily*. She wanted to tell the story of Dakota people and to re-create life in the camp circle before the Europeans came. She wrote to her friend Margaret Mead that she hoped the novel would appeal to many readers. "Only my characters are imaginary," she said. "And it is purely the woman's point of view, her problems, aspirations."

For two years, Deloria worked on the story of Blue Bird and her daughter, Waterlily. Her friend Ruth Benedict helped edit it. The novel showed how Dakota women shared knowledge with their children as they grew up. By 1948, shortly before Benedict's death, the manuscript was ready to publish. Deloria submitted the book to several publishers, all of whom turned it down. They said people were no longer interested in reading about Dakota life.

After finishing *Waterlily*, she had to find new ways to support herself and Susan. More than anything, she wanted to keep writing and collecting stories from Dakota people. She raised enough funds to work on a new manuscript, *Dakota Family Life: Social Patterns and Education*. This book shared more of her research on kinship and family life.

In 1955, Deloria and Susan were hired to run St. Elizabeth's, the school they had attended as young girls. Then the University of South Dakota hired Deloria in 1961 to be the assistant director of the W. H. Over Museum. Her job was to study the Dakota language. With the support of a grant, an award of funds, she also worked on a Dakota dictionary.

Susan passed away in 1963. Deloria was sad to lose her sister and companion after so many years together, but she was determined to keep working. Already in her seventies, she learned to drive so she could interview elders at remote reservations.

She kept working until she became ill from a stroke. Deloria died in 1971, in Wagner, South Dakota, not far from where she was born on the Yankton Reservation. She was buried at St. Philip's Church along with her sister, mother, grandmother, and other relatives. Her nephew, Vine Deloria Jr., said, "In death as in life, Ella was surrounded by family."

In all the ways that matter most, Ella Cara Deloria lived a good life. As a Dakota woman, she followed the kinship rules and cultural values that were important to her. Through all the challenges she faced, Deloria kept writing, recording stories, and taking care of her family.

After forty years, while typing with only nine fingers, Deloria wrote sixteen different publications.

She created several pageants that performed Native stories. Writing about kinship and women's roles became one of her most important contributions to the study of Dakota culture.

Waterlily was not published until 1988, seventeen years after Deloria's death. Since then, it has become a treasured book that shows the beautiful life Dakota people had created. Her book helps people today learn about Dakota culture. She left behind many unpublished stories and manuscripts that are stored in various archives. Her *Dakota Family Life* manuscript was finally published in 2007 as *The Dakota Way of Life*.

To honor Deloria's work, Columbia University created the Ella C. Deloria Undergraduate Research Fellowship in 2010. St. Mary's School in South Dakota offers a scholarship for a senior girl who carries on the Dakota way of life as shown in her work.

Throughout her life, Ella Cara Deloria remained true to the vision that began with her grandfather, Saswe. In a changing world filled with danger and great opportunities, Deloria's hard work and sacrifices helped preserve the Dakota way of life.

Historical Context

The Dakota and Ojibwe people have histories as rich and full of struggle as the US or other countries. This timeline presents important events in one place as a reminder that no one human history is more important than another, but history often makes it look that way. This timeline also provides context from the Dakota and Ojibwe histories. You can use it to respond to the book by comparing the timelines of each person featured in this series to the events listed here.

Beyond memory, this place called Mni Sota Makoce, or Minnesota, is where the people became Dakota. They traveled as far north as Hudson's Bay in Canada, as far west as the Rocky Mountains, south to trade with the Pueblos, and to the southeast past the trading city of Cahokia to the southeastern part of what became the United States.

During this same time, Anishinaabeg, the larger group that includes Ojibwe people, lived far to the east of Minnesota, near the Atlantic Ocean. A series of prophecies, or visions of their future, set the Ojibwe off on their five-hundred-year journey to find a new home in "a land where food grows on water" (meaning manoomin, wild rice) along the Great Lakes and eventually in Minnesota.

Timeline

900–1400	The Dakota live, as they have always, in what will become Minnesota; ancestors of other Indigenous groups, including the Ojibwe, begin migrating west.
1540–1622	Spanish and French explorers map the Mississippi River and Dakota village sites and make contact with the Ojibwe at Lake Superior.
1730–1850	Ojibwe and Dakota fight over Dakota territories; battles end with their peace agreement in 1870, which remains unbroken.
1776–1783	The American Revolution is fought.
1805	The Dakota agree to sell land to the US government, but the US government never pays.
1816	**Saswe, Ella Cara Deloria's grandfather, is born in what is now Minnesota.**
1819	Fort St. Anthony, renamed Fort Snelling in 1825, is built at Bdote (meeting place of rivers in present-day St. Paul, Minnesota).
1825	The Dakota and Ojibwe lose land in the Prairie du Chien treaty.
1830	Congress passes the Indian Removal Act, forcing all Native Americans to move west of the Mississippi River.
1837–1850s	Treaties force the Dakota and Ojibwe onto reservations, and they lose hundreds of millions of acres of homeland.

1849–1857 Minnesota Territory is established, and American settlers encroach on Dakota lands.

1858 Minnesota becomes a state.

1861–1865 The American Civil War is fought.

1862 War between the Dakota and the US begins in August and ends in September.

1863 The US repeals treaties, and almost all Dakota are removed from Minnesota.

1880s The Dakota people begin to return to their communities in Minnesota.

1884 The Haskell Institute opens as a boarding school for Native American children.

1889 Ella Cara Deloria is born on the Yankton Reservation in South Dakota.

1914 Deloria graduates from Columbia University with a bachelor's degree in education.

1924 Congress passes the Indian Citizenship Act, granting citizenship to all Native Americans.

1927 Deloria teaches at Haskell.

1953 The US makes laws to end the legal status of tribes as nations during the years known as the Termination era.

1956 The Indian Relocation Act passes to move Native Americans off reservations to cities.

1971 Deloria dies in South Dakota.

1978 The American Indian Religious Freedom Act ends the outlaw of a tribe's religious and cultural practices.

1988 Deloria's *Waterlily* is published.

2007 Deloria's *The Dakota Way of Life* is published.

Glossary

anthropologist: a person who carries out research in the field of anthropology, the study of human beings or human nature

dialect: a form or variety of a language of a specific region in respect to vocabulary, pronunciation, and other ways of speech

ethnologist: an expert in or student of ethnology, the branch of knowledge concerned with human society and culture and the development and characteristics of a group of people

immigrant: a person who comes to settle permanently in another country or region, as viewed from the perspective of those already living in that land

kinship: ties of relationship by birth, marriage, or ritual that form the basis of social organization

linguist: a person who is skilled in the learning or use of languages; a person who specializes in the structure or historical development of one of more languages; an interpreter or translator

missionary: a person sent on a religious mission to convert people to Christianity; relating to the work of a mission or the building housing mission workers or teachers

off-reservation boarding school: a government-run school where Native American children lived from grade school through high school and sometimes year-round. A few of these schools remain open.

oral: relating to communication by speech; relating to a tradition, culture, society, etc., in which the spoken word is the chief form of communication and shared from generation to generation

reservation: an area of land held and governed by a Native American tribal nation

Source Notes

15 Vine Deloria Jr., *Singing for a Spirit: A Portrait of the Dakota Sioux* (Santa Fe, NM: Clear Light, 1999), 45.

33 Ella Cara Deloria, *Waterlily* (Lincoln: University of Nebraska Press, 1988), 238.

33 Deloria, 237.

35 Ella Cara Deloria, letter to Franz Boas, February 7, 1936, Franz Boas Professional Papers, LH-B-14-2, American Philosophical Society, Philadelphia.

37 Ella Cara Deloria, letter to Franz Boas, June 11, 1932.

39 Ella Cara Deloria, *Speaking of Indians* (Lincoln: University of Nebraska Press, 1998), 70.

41 Deloria, *Waterlily*, vi.

43 Deloria, *Speaking of Indians*, xix.

Extend Your Learning

IDEAS FOR WRITING AND DISCUSSION

- What moment in this story do you think you will most remember? Why?
- Who do you believe was most important to this person's success? Why?
- What do you think were the hardest moments for this person? Why?
- How do you think this person was able to overcome hardship in their life?
- What were the happiest moments in the story of this person's life?
- What moment in the story reminded you of something in your own life?
- Write your own short autobiography, the story of your life so far!

IDEAS FOR VISUAL PROJECTS

- Draw images for three or four moments that are not illustrated in this book.
- Draw a sketch of this person and include items they liked.
- Find images from American Indian boarding schools from the time this book covers.
- Find historic images to share of activities this book mentions. Are they different now?
- Find historic images to share of the reservations or places this book mentions.

- Make a map of tribal nations near where you live. Where are reservations located? What tribes live there? What else did you learn about these tribal nations?

- Create a bar graph, pie chart, or other infographic on one of these topics:

    1. How many Native Americans live in urban areas near you? Which US cities are home to the largest populations of Native Americans?
    2. How many Native American students are there in your school district? How many tribes are represented?
    3. Explore "Why Treaties Matter" and give a brief report about how treaties formed the reservations and the homelands of Dakota and Ojibwe peoples.

Resources for Visual Projects
American Indian Education: Teaching and Learning
https://education.mn.gov/MDE/dse/indian/teach/

Why Treaties Matter
https://treatiesmatter.org/exhibit/

IDEAS FOR FURTHER LEARNING

The Dakota and Ojibwe people continue to live in Minnesota and are part of all aspects of our society. While English is a shared language, many Dakota and Ojibwe people also study and speak Dakota and Anishinaabemowin, their Indigenous languages.

- Find unfamiliar words in this book, and create a glossary or word list with definitions.

- Create a timeline for this person's life.

- Learn how to count to ten in Dakota or Ojibwe.
- Look up Ojibwe or Dakota words for baseball or other ball games such as lacrosse.
- Learn about Dakota and Ojibwe sports and activities such as powwows.
- Make a list of four common traditions the Ojibwe and Dakota share.

Resources to Learn More

Historic Fort Snelling: Educator Resources
https://www.mnhs.org/fortsnelling/learn/educator-resources

Minnesota Historical Society: Beginning Dakota
http://beginningdakota.org

Minnesota Historical Society: Minnesota Territory
http://www.mnhs.org/talesoftheterritory

Minnesota Historical Society: Ojibwe Material Culture
http://www.mnhs.org/ojibwematerialculture

The Ojibwe People's Dictionary
https://ojibwe.lib.umn.edu

About the Author

Diane Wilson is a Dakota author, educator, and bog steward. Her novel, *The Seed Keeper* (2021), and her memoir, *Spirit Car: Journey to a Dakota Past* (2006), won the Minnesota Book Awards in 2022 and 2007, respectively. She has also published a nonfiction book, *Beloved Child*, and coauthored a picture book—*Where We Come From*. Her essays have appeared in anthologies including *Kinship: Belonging in a World of Relations* (2021), *We Are Meant to Rise* (2021), and *A Good Time for the Truth* (2016). She is the former executive director for Dream of Wild Health and the Native American Food Sovereignty Alliance. In addition to this book, she authored other books in this series. Wilson is a Mdewakanton descendant, enrolled on the Rosebud Reservation.

About the Illustrator

Tashia Hart is an author and illustrator; her works include *Native Love Jams* (2023), *The Good Berry Cookbook: Harvesting and Cooking Wild Rice and Other Wild Foods* (2021), *Gidjie and the Wolves* (2020), and *Girl Unreserved* (2015). She was assistant illustrator for *Gaa-pi-izhiwebak* (2021) and illustrator for *Gidjie and the Wolves* (2020). Her short works include recipes, essays, poetry, and short stories for various publications. In addition to this title, she has also illustrated several of the books in this series. She is a citizen of the Red Lake Nation and resides in Duluth, Minnesota.

About the Series Editors

Heid E. Erdrich is a member of the Ojibwe Nation enrolled at the Turtle Mountain Reservation in North Dakota. She grew up in Wahpeton, North Dakota. She is also German American and Metis from Canada. Erdrich has written several books of poetry and a cookbook focused on Indigenous foods. Along with being Anishinaabe/Ojibwe, Erdrich's extended family includes Dakota, Hidatsa, Somali American, German American, and immigrants from India. She loves the stories of how many kinds of people came to call one place home. Erdrich has lived in Minnesota for many years, raising her kids in Minneapolis, where they went to public schools.

Gwen N. Westerman is Dakota from the Sisseton Wahpeton Oyate and a citizen of the Cherokee Nation of Oklahoma. She grew up in Kansas among many different tribal nations. Today, she writes about Dakota history, and writes poetry in English and Dakota. Westerman's ancestors were teachers, leaders, and hard workers who were Dakota, Cherokee, Ojibwe, and Odawa along with a few French and Scottish traders. She lives in Minnesota, where her kids grew up playing ice hockey and soccer.